Sailor

MW00364348

Written by Jill Eggleton
Illustrated by Jim Storey

Sam was a sailor
on a big boat.
But he was not like
the other sailors.

He couldn't get up the mast.

He couldn't clean the deck.

The sailors laughed at Sam.
"You're not a sailor,"
they said.

3

The captain went to see Sam.
"Go to Sailor School," she said.
"Come back when you can
be a sailor."

So Sam got off the boat
and went up the road
to look for Sailor School.

Sam saw a big building.
There were people
going in and out.
They had buckets
and brooms.
They had ropes and ladders.

"This must be a school
for sailors," said Sam.
So he went in.

So Sam sat on a chair
and fell off!

He put water on his head.

"Wow!" said the sailors.
"We're going to
Sailor School!"
And they got off the boat.

"Come back!"
shouted the captain.
"I don't want clowns
for sailors!"

But the sailors were singing . . .

A Comic Strip

Sailor Sam

Guide Notes

Title: Sailor Sam
Stage: Early (3) – Blue

Genre: Fiction
Approach: Guided Reading
Processes: Thinking Critically, Exploring Language, Processing Information
Written and Visual Focus: Comic Strip

THINKING CRITICALLY
(sample questions)
- What do you think this story could be about?
- What do you know about sailors?
- What sort of things do sailors have to be good at doing?
- Look at pages 2 and 3. Why do you think the sailors are laughing at Sam?
- Look at pages 4 and 5. Why don't you think the captain wants Sam on the boat?
- Look at pages 6 and 7. Why does Sam think that this is a school for sailors?
- Look at pages 12 and 13. Why do you think the other sailors are getting off the boat?
- Look at page 14. Why do you think the captain is upset?

EXPLORING LANGUAGE

Terminology
Title, cover, illustrations, author, illustrator

Vocabulary
Interest words: sailor, mast, deck, captain
High-frequency words (new): other, boat, teacher, road, let
Positional words: on, off, up

Print Conventions
Capital letter for sentence beginnings and names (**S**am), periods, exclamation marks, quotation marks, commas, ellipses